CATCHING UP ON CATECHETICS

Catching Up on Catechetics

by
Albert J. Shamon

PAULIST PRESS
New York / Paramus / Toronto

NIHIL OBSTAT:
Francis B. Burns
Censor Deputatus

IMPRIMATUR:
✠Joseph L. Hogan, D.D., S.T.D.
Bishop of Rochester

June 17, 1972

The Nihil Obstat and Imprimatur are official declarations that a book or pamphlet is free of doctrinal or moral error. No implication is contained therein that those who have granted the Nihil Obstat and Imprimatur agree with the contents, opinions or statements expressed.

Copyright © 1972 by
The Missionary Society
of St. Paul the Apostle
in the State of New York

Library of Congress
Catalog Card Number: 72-85698

ISBN 0-8091-1739-8

Published by Paulist Press
Editorial Office: 1865 Broadway, N.Y., N.Y. 10023
Business Office: 400 Sette Drive, Paramus, N.J. 07652

Printed and bound in the
United States of America

Contents

Preface 9

Components of Religious Education 11

Catechetics: An Adventure in Discovering 27

Catechetics: A Process 35

Films in the Catechetical Process 43

Catechetical Aim: Conscience Formation 53

The General Catechetical Directory 63

Appendix 1: On Definitions 69

Appendix 2: Analyses of Some Catechetical Films 73

Author's Prenote

The first essay appeared in *Guide*, No. 299, June-July, 1968 (Published by The Missionary Society of St. Paul the Apostle, N.Y., N.Y. 10025). The second and third essays appeared in *Religion Teacher's Journal,* February and May/June, 1972 (Twenty-Third Publications, P.O. Box 180, West Mystic, Connecticut 06388).

I wish to express my deep appreciation to Mr. Joseph Weber who proofread the manuscript with me and contributed many valuable suggestions. Also, I wish to thank Dolores Dennis who typed the manuscript.

Albert J. Shamon
March 1972

"What is needed is that this certain and immutable doctrine, to which we owe obedience, be studied afresh and reformulated in contemporary terms. For this deposit of faith . . . is one thing; the manner in which these truths are set forth . . . is something else."

John XXIII
Opening Address to Vatican Council II

Preface

One of the major causes of criticism regarding new catechetical textbooks is due to ignorance of the catechetical method underlying them. Because so few teachers really understand the principles behind the new catechetics, the textbooks are either misused or discarded. So many teachers still commonly equate religious education to imparting information as is done in any academic subject. Other teachers use only a part of the new methods—such as audio-visuals and group dynamics—without seeing these as only a part of the catechetical process.

Because of these all too common errors, there has been a crying need for a lucid presentation of the proper method undergirding the new catechetics. *Catching Up on Catechetics* strives to do just that. It gives first an overview of religious education in general. Then it quickly proceeds to explain in two chapters the catechetical process. Once the process is explained, the book points out how modern instructional aids are meant to fit into this process and thus make their best contribution to religious education.

Because the aim of religious education is to assist the individual to form his conscience and because I have discovered that so many teachers did not seem to understand what this implied, an entire chapter has been devoted to conscience formation.

This new approach to catechetics has been an outgrowth of the spirit of Vatican II. The General Catechetical Directory, released by Rome in 1971, confirms this concept of catechetics as process. Hence a short history of the Directory and a brief analysis of its content is included in a final chapter.

Two appendices are added: one stating the place of definition in catechetics historically and according to the Director; and the second an analysis of some current catechetical films in the light of the catechetical process that hopefully will prove helpful to teachers.

The book purposely was kept concise to bring out essentials and to be able to be fitted into the busy time-schedules of teachers. It will be of value to all teachers using the new catechetical methods, but especially to those familiar with the *Come to the Father* Program. For the same reason this book will be a boon to all parents who take seriously their responsibility in sharing the religious education of their children.

Albert J. Shamon

Components of Religious Education

O'Henry in his short story "The Third Ingredient" wrote that everyone knew that a good stew has three ingredients: meat, potatoes, and an onion. So every catechist should know that good religious education has three elements: one from the present, one from the past, and one from the future. Religious education is the product of three components: the *present* —the Church community: worshiping and teaching; the *past*—its heritage; and the *future*—its mission.

I suppose it would be good to start with a definition of what religious education is. To put it simply, *religious education is the handing on of the faith from generation to generation* (2 Tim. 1:12-13; 2 Thess. 2:15). For after all, why does the Church exist, why does the parish exist, why does the school exist? Is it not to spread the faith, to deepen the faith, to celebrate the faith? Could not our Lord write across almost every page of the Gospel, "I want faith"? In other words, the whole problem of religious education revolves around faith: it is the tradition of faith. But before we can hand it on, we must first know what faith is.

The Reformers seemed to downplay the intellectual content of faith. They often stressed emotionalism, the I've-got-faith revivalism, the enthusiasm, of Wesley. In reaction, the Church insisted on the intellectuality of faith. She protested that faith is an assent of the intellect, under the movement of grace, to the truths revealed by God. And as almost always happens in polemics, we read more into what the Church said than she meant. We reduced faith to just an act of the intellect, and religious education—the handing on of the faith—to the imparting of a body of truths. We reduced religious education to information and religious teaching to instruction. This was, to say the least, a violation of the integrity of man. We divided man, like Gaul, into three parts: body, soul, and intellect. Man is a man—a single, undivided person. He thinks, yes. But his thinking involves him totally: his feelings, his desires, his actions, himself.

Faith Is the Response of a Person to a Person

Before faith is an intellectual assent to truths, it is a response to a person. The Word of God is a living Person, not an abstraction; not something but Someone! When we say we have faith in somebody, what do we really mean? We mean we believe in him—believe in him, not just with our heads, but with all our heart and soul and strength. And because we believe in him, we trust him and accept all he says. In other words, faith arrows first to the person and then, and only then, to his message.

Components of Religious Education

For instance, suppose we are stranded on a desert island a-la-Robinson Crusoe. We wait, we hope, we pray for deliverance. Week follows week, and our desire begins to wane, to border on despair. Then one day someone calls to us. What is our instant reaction? We don't sit down and first analyze what he is saying, do we? A voice to us means only one thing —a person, somebody. And in these particular circumstances, the voice brings with it hope, salvation, rescue. What is our first response? Is it not joy? The voice says in effect, "I bring you news of great joy." Our next reaction is to race and leap with joy into the arms of the person who called out. Only after that do we finally get around to listening to how our rescuer chanced to find us and why he came to this island, and how he will save us.

And so faith is first a person's response—the response of our total selves, not just our intellects—to a Person, not just to truths about him.

> Not What, but Whom!
>   For Christ is more than all the creeds,
>   And His full life of gentle deeds
>   Shall all the creeds outlive.
> Not what I do believe,
> But Whom!
> Not what,
> But Whom!
>
> John Oxenham, "Credo"

Thus we say, "I believe IN God," not "I believe God." Because I believe in God, I believe Him and everything He tells me. Faith in a person precedes intellectual assent to truths.

What does all this mean in regard to religious education?

First of all it confirms what we already have said, namely, that religious education must be more than instruction—for faith is more than the response of the intellect to truths. Faith is a personal encounter, between a living God and a living man, like that between God and Abraham in Ur of the Chaldees. Therefore, faith is first of all a long, long process. For persons do not get to know each other at the first encounter. Thus young couples, taking each other seriously, must go steady. Aristotle said that to become friends, persons must eat a bushel of salt together—that is, must have many, many meals together. Religious education, therefore, must never be equated with, or limited to, Catholic schooling. The two are not identical. Schooling begins with school. But religious education must begin at birth—at the moment the child can respond to his environment—and it continues to deepen past adolescence and old age. In other words, religious education is a cradle-to-grave affair. Therefore, the Catholic school is not at all the major part of the religious education picture, although it is a mighty important part of that picture. Pre-school and post-school education are equally important. In the future, we shall have to see that our resources are more proportionately expended to the pre-school and adult levels of Christian growth as well as to the school age level.

Christian Community

In the second place, since faith is a personal response to Persons, it is basically a relationship and an experience—an experiential relationship. Therefore, the role of the Christian community is all-important in religious education. Only in a community are interpersonal relationships possible. Only through interpersonal relationships can one become a person, fully human. How does a child learn before it goes to school? By living in the community of the family. A child learns more from its living at home than from its instructions there. Instructions are important, but at that age level, not so important as the teaching and learning that goes on with living.

Christ established His kingdom on earth as a family. In the New Testament the word used to describe what happens to persons in the Christian faith is "adoption," and adoption suggests a family, a community—one is adopted by a family. Baptism is the sacrament of adoption, the entrance into the Christian community. As the child begins to assimilate the traditions and heritage of the family from the moment of its adoption, so religious education begins from the moment of baptism. And this handing on of the faith, which is religious education, is sought in the Christian community. When the parents bring the baby to be baptized, the priest's first question is, "What do you ask of God's Church for N?" And they answer, "Faith." The child comes to the Christian community for faith. If the Christian community does not have faith, will the child have faith? The Christian community is a worshiping and a teaching community. In Acts 2:42, after Pentecost had given the apostles new insights into the faith, we read of the early Christian community that "they continued steadfastly in prayer, the teaching of the apostles and the breaking of the bread. . . ."

Teaching Community

We are not concerned here with the worshiping Christian community but with the teaching Christian community—the school. How best can the school transmit the faith? In grades one to three, I would say perhaps quite formally, for the child needs proper direction and orientation. But once the child's steps are turned in the right direction, then in the intermediate years, let us say grades four to seven, his faith should be allowed to grow in the way best suited to the child at this age level—namely, by his experiencing it, by living in a truly Christian community. The child must meet Christ at this level, not so much in textbooks as in persons. A spirit is caught quicker than taught. Christ must become a living reality, and He can only through living persons. Christianity must become a living experience, and it can only through a Christian community of persons. In the Parable of the Sower, where did Christ put the stress? Was it not on the soil, the environment, the milieu, the community in which the seed lives?

Hence, Gabriel Moran has made a startling suggestion. He advocates no formal religious instruction in the middle elementary years. In an article "Religion Is for Adults" he says, speaking of the intermediate years:

". . . children ought simply be allowed to grow up. The Catholic school ought to provide a truly human and Christian atmosphere in which they can grow. . . . THE MILIEU IS THE CHIEF FORMATIVE INFLUENCE, and the function of the Catholic school at this level is to be a 'citadel of charity.' "

In fact, this is one of the best arguments for Catholic schools, yet the one least used—namely, it is able to create a Christian community where the child can get a Catholic mind almost by the process of osmosis. This means not that there should be no religious instruction in grades four to seven, but that it need not be formal instruction. In the home the child is taught, is he not, by word or explanation, given as the occasion arises, as well as by example? So in these intermediate years the faith, lived by the Christian community of the school and taught as the occasion arises, would inculcate right attitudes and ideals far better than mere book learning. And Christian attitudes at this age are more important than right answers.

I say this not as necessarily endorsing the dropping of formal religious instruction in grades four to seven, but rather to set minds at ease when current religious textbooks seem devoid of definition or seem nebulous.

Twofold Defect

The great fault with religious education in the past, if there were fault, is, as I see it, twofold: (1) we reduced it to definitions, and (2) we tried to impart too much.

As for definitions, they are the culmination of

knowledge. Only after one knows a thing perfectly can he define it. Definition is the last step in the learning process. And some would put it first. (See Appendix 1.)

Piaget conducted many studies on the development of thinking. He presented a great deal of evidence to support the conclusion that formal thought does not appear until eleven or twelve years of age.

The Stanford-Binet and Wechsler intelligence test booklets pointed to the same conclusion: "Conceptual thinking, in a consistent and sustained way, before eleven to thirteen years of age is not possible."

Piaget, Gesell, Kohlberg, and Brunner caused Robert O'Neill and Father Donovan in a paper on "Psychological Development and the Concept of Mortal Sin" to conclude that the "age of reason," defined in terms of cognitive development sufficient to enable the child to comprehend concepts, group relationships, and understand distinctions, occurs at the onset of adolescence—that is, between eleven and thirteen years of age in most children. (How true! A child for instance, who has not been to confession for six months, can tell little more than the "sins" of the day or the morning before.)

As for doctrinal content, we gave the child too much. We cultivated in teachers an agenda anxiety—a feverish fear that we must cover all the matter of religion in grammar school or else all is lost—as though the salvation of the student depended on that. What we labor so painstakingly to inject in the fifth grade could be picked up easily and readily at a higher level, when it would be more meaningful. If it is not meaningful at the fifth grade level, is not the child apt to think that religion will not be meaningful at any other level?

So the first great ingredient in religious education is the living Christian community, making Christ visible and present in teacher and pupils—giving the child the one lesson he best can learn at this age: the lesson from experience.

Progressive Discovery

The second component of religious education regards the past: it is the appropriation of our Christian heritage. Christian faith expresses itself in beliefs and doctrines. But this expression or definition of our faith is the final step in a threefold process. Faith begins with an event, not with a doctrine. Christianity began with an event, not a philosophy; with Somebody, not something. The event evokes the response of faith. Faith lived is finally formulated. Thus Israel's faith began with the Exodus-event: God's intervention in behalf of His people; Christian faith began with the resurrection-event: Christ's passing from death to life. These interventions were followed by the response of faith—belief in the Person encountered. Only later came the formulation of that faith: the Passover narrations that crystallized into much of the Old Testament, and the faith of the early Christian communities that was later embodied in the four Gospels. We, however, tended to reverse this process. We formulated the faith first; then we defined it for the child; and then we hopefully expected that somehow he would live up to the definitions. Then, finally, maybe he would experience the Christ-event.

But even in this second aspect of religious education—the appropriation of our Christian heritage—again the aim is not indoctrination, to hand out packaged information. In the Passover celebration, there comes a point in the meal when the youngest child asks the head of the home what is the feast all about. The father replies by narrating the history of Israel. But note: the child is already experiencing the Passover event. Similarly, religious education must be the appropriation of a heritage being already lived out by the child—living, praying, and worshiping in the Christian community. Hence religious education should be programmed for discovery rather than for instruction. The aim is CONVERSION, an actual change of heart and mind.

God's Interior Action

Conversion requires, besides the patience of the teacher and the prayerfulness of both teacher and students, interior action on the part of God, for He alone can illumine minds and change hearts. This is what Paul said when he wrote to his Corinthians, "I planted the seed and Apollos watered it, but God made it grow" (1 Cor. 3:6).

The third component of religious education regards the future: religious education is for mission. The Christian community is by nature missionary. The faith is not given to us for hoarding. The man who buried his talent lost it. Israel was chosen, not for privilege, but for mission—she was to be a light of revelation to the Gentiles. When she was not, God rejected her; and His Son chose in her place the

Twelve—not from the rabbinical schools, nor from Jewish officialdom, but from the unlettered, the untutored, fishermen! He would not put new wine in old wineskins. He chose twelve to symbolize that here was a new Israel—again chosen for mission: to be a light of revelation to the Gentiles. "I am come to cast fire on the earth, and what would I but that it be enkindled."

Rev. Richard Wurmbrand in his book *Tortured for Christ* wrote: "We should never stop at having won a soul for Christ. By this, you have done only half the work. Every soul won for Christ must be made to be a soul-winner" (p. 16).

A Faith Shared

Speaking of the instructions given to young communists, Douglas Hyde wrote: "He will be made to feel, right from the start of the very first session, that instruction is not an end in itself. . . . He is made to understand that the knowledge he gains will be . . . something to be used, not just absorbed. And he can see that this is not just words, for all around him are people who are living the Communism he is being taught" (*Dedication and Leadership*, p. 49). It was Lenin who said that "theory without action is sterile; and action without theory is stupid."

Father Gerard Sloyan wrote in *Christ the Lord:* "If we don't spread the good news about Christ's victory over death and sin, it soon stops meaning much to us. . . . We don't pray enough—to the Holy Spirit for light and guidance. We don't read enough—of God's love for us in the Bible. We, twentieth century disciples, don't fulfill our duty of confirmation enough—by telling the good news to others" (pp. 15-16).

This missionary aspect of religious education has been the facet of education most neglected. The great fault of religious education in the past has been that it was too INTROVERTED. Concerned about developing Christian character and Christian institutions, it too often drew persons out of the world instead of driving them into the world, where Christian witness and service could mean something.

It was this aspect of religious education that Bishop Sheen was most concerned about when, as Bishop of the Diocese of Rochester, he ordered a revision of the administration of the sacrament of Confirmation. In his letter on this matter Bishop Sheen spoke of three views of the world.

Church and World

The Church before Vatican I (1870) viewed the world as evil, as tantamount to worldliness. And she saw herself seated apart from it, proudly on a mountaintop, secure in her retreat, a bulwark, a mighty fortress, defending herself against the world. Once in a while she would send out a "scalping party" to get converts and bring them back to safety within her embrace.

Before Vatican II (1962) the Church saw the world as a pie cut into sectors: one to herself, one to the political sphere, one to the economic, and so on. The Church was related to the world only as a sector

Components of Religious Education

of it. Pius XI sought to leaven the other sectors by Catholic Action.

After Vatican II, the Church sees the world as a circle and herself as permeating it. The world in this view was not looked upon as something evil, but as a cosmos, a thing of beauty; as God's creation and so something good; something to be divinized and transformed. A world from which God did not remain aloof, but entered and risked His life to leaven. Father Bernard Cooke calls this an experiential faith: a sharing with others of our faith in Christ (*The Challenge of Vatican II,* p. 37).

Therefore, Christ did two things. His first word was "Come, follow me." He gathered His apostles, took them out of the world—to educate them. His last word was "Go, teach all nations." The purpose of the gathering was for mission.

All religious education must have this ultimate orientation. Just as the seminary courses are all pointed to the priesthood, so all religious education should be pointed to Confirmation. As ordination is but the beginning of a priest's mission, so Confirmation, the climax of the lay priesthood, is the official deputation of the layman to go out and bring God to the world and the world to God.

Some Protestant churches are already structuring their religion courses so that they will ultimately evoke this response of Christian commitment in Confirmation. Only religious education for mission can fit one to make an act of confirmation like this one demanded by these churches.

Confirmation Dialogue

Leader: As through this Love Feast you are joined anew to God, so you are delivered from yourself, and from those powers which would make a slave of you. What are you delivered to? Is there a purpose in God's deliverance of you?

People: Yes. I am freed from myself for the world. Jesus Christ declares me to be a free person, but I am freed for a mission to the world. I am called to love that world, even as I am loved, knowing that I am not alone, but that God suffers with me in the midst of the world. God is waiting for me in the midst of it all, waiting for me to come. Each moment of every day He is waiting for me to be about His business, down Main Street, a country road, a slum alley, thirty floors up in an apartment building, on a tractor thirty acres from nowhere, in Mississippi, in the church building.

Leader: It is a world filled with the pain of birth and death, paralyzed by the anxiety of life; a world that cries out! Do you hear the world's cries?

People: Yes, I do.

Leader: Will you respond to those cries?

People: Yes, I will.

Leader: How will you respond to the cries of the world?

People: By the giving of myself in service.

Leader: And how will you give yourself in service?

People: I will go into the world and love. I am weak, yet God's love makes me strong. Though I may be despised, yet I will love, for I know the love that can heal and restore. I will go into the world and love.

Components of Religious Education

Wouldn't it be wonderful for our religious education to be so geared as to climax in such a commitment!

To sum up, religious education involves three things:

LIVING THE FAITH: that is, getting involved in the Christian community: worshiping and teaching.

LEARNING THE FAITH: that is, appropriating the Christian heritage, through formal teaching.

LEAVENING THE WORLD: that is, getting involved in the world to transform it.

In conclusion, let us meditate a moment on one of Israel's most educated Jews, Saul of Tarsus. Saul was proud of his traditional religion. He was so sure of himself. He detested all innovation. Then Christ came.

Saul had his own ideas of God. Jesus—a common carpenter—did not fit in with them. Jesus was unorthodox, and Saul's religion was the orthodox one. Indignant, Saul persecuted the followers of Jesus. Saul had so well defined God, he no longer took the trouble to listen to Him. He became a fanatic.

The only way to change the mind of a fanatic is to use lightning. In a flash, Saul was blinded, converted. His catechism was a single sentence, the revelation of a Person: "I am Jesus whom you are persecuting." Saul learned that God was not just a doctrine, studied and imposed, but a living Person—Jesus. Not a Jesus way up there, but a Jesus right down here, who could be persecuted. Not a stranger Jesus, but a Jesus who knew his name, "Saul, Saul."

Saul, who was to evangelize the nations, learned that he had to beg instructions from a simple disciple, Ananias, whose only superiority over Saul was that he belonged to the Christian community. The hand of God made Paul blind, but it was from the hands of a believer that he was to recover his sight. Even the weakest of us can hand on the faith. But it is a long, long process—a deep, deep experience. In fact, faith is a life spent in discovering God.

Catechetics: An Adventure in Discovering

In the past few years, new catechetical texts and procedures have appeared and have generated widespread opposition to their content and methods. Now that the majority of teachers are using such texts, we can discuss what all this "newness" is about. There is an Oriental proverb that says, "When you give a man a fish, you give him strength to live for a day; but when you teach a man how to fish, you give him the ability to live for a lifetime." Once parents and teachers transcend the apparent problems of particular lessons and understand the rationale undergirding these texts and methods, the lessons themselves will make sense, and fears about orthodoxy will be laid to rest.

Recall the story of the two disciples on the road to Emmaus as told by St. Luke (24:13-25). These two disciples had followed Christ for years. They had hoped He would free their nation from Roman domination. Then on a Friday called good, they saw Him die. He was buried. On Sunday some women told them that they had seen Him risen. But the disciples had not. So their hopes were still dashed to the ground. Thus on the first Easter Sunday, they were trudging home to pick up the pieces. As they walked, a stranger appeared out of nowhere. He asked, "Why are you sad?" He listened with His heart as well as with His ears.

The two sensed His empathy, so they opened up and told Him the whole story of the last three days.

When they were finished, He began to speak. " 'What little sense you have,' He said. 'Did not the Messiah have to undergo all this so as to enter into His glory?' Beginning, then, with Moses and all the prophets, He interpreted every passage of Scripture which referred to Him." What had looked to them like the end now began to loom up like a beginning. Their hearts were burning within them.

At their journey's end, they begged the stranger to stay with them. He did. "When He had seated Himself with them to eat, He took bread, pronounced the blessing, then broke the bread and began to distribute it to them. *With that their eyes were opened.* . . ." He had been with them all along the road. He could have told them who He was right from the start. Instead, He let them discover Him. After their discovery, they hurried back to the apostles and themselves became apostles.

This Easter event illustrates beautifully the new catechetical process. If we analyze the event, we shall discover that it is composed of four parts. First, there was the *human experience:* being with Christ for a few years and especially witnessing His death and burial. Then there was the *Christian message:* Christ teaching them from Scripture on the way to

Catechetics: An Adventure in Discovering

Emmaus. Next in the breaking of the bread came the *discovery*. Finally came the *response* in aligning themselves once more with the apostles.

In what way does this process differ from the old catechetical method? In the old teaching model the focus was on the teacher. He had all the knowledge and passed it on to the student who was supposed not to have it. The content was the presentation of truths. The process was the lecture. And the product was to gain an intellectual assent or rejection of the truths based on the authority of the teacher or the evidence of the facts presented.

But the transmission of knowledge does not confer learning on a student any more than a depositor makes a teller rich merely by handing over his money to him. Or to change the analogy, having food set before one does not nourish him. One must eat and digest it.

To learn, one must possess, make his own, assimilate and digest the facts and truths transmitted. Therefore, the emphasis has shifted to a new teaching model, the present one employed in the new catechetical texts.

In the new model, the focus is on the student—his learning—not on the teacher. The content of the teaching is not just the presentation of truths; it is the presentation of one person to another, the proclamation of the good news of salvation. The process consists in probing a life experience in the light of the Christian message. And this calls for more than a mere intellectual assent; it is an invitation to change one's life. The product, therefore, is the transformation of the child. And the method is the fourfold one used by Christ Himself.

CHART I

	FOCUS	CONTENT	PROCESS	PRODUCT
Old Model	TEACHER	TRUTHS	LECTURE	INTELLECTUAL ASSENT ONLY
New Model	STUDENT	PERSONS	PROBING EXPERIENCE	CONVERSION

Thus the new catechetics takes a slice of life, a human experience. Either it creates this by a film, or it has the child recall one or experience one in the classroom. The teacher's role is that of enabler or facilitator; that is, the teacher helps the student probe this experience. In fact, most of a class, or even more than one class, may be spent on this single phase. The experience of the Emmaus disciples was a many-year one with Christ.

In the seventh grade text of the *Come to the Father* series, two entire classes are spent on probing the meaning of departure. "Kids" talk about moving, going camping, changes in their growth, in their thinking, in their feelings, in their choosing. All this is by way of preparation for the sacrament of Baptism as a departure experience, a Christian exodus, a call by God to leave behind a former way of life and assume a new one.

After the experience is probed, the Christian message is proclaimed, often from Scripture or liturgy or dogma or witness. Christ on the way to Emmaus used Scripture; the seventh grade text uses the liturgy of Baptism and the call of Abraham to illumine

Catechetics: An Adventure in Discovering 31

the human experience of departure.

After this comes the discovery. The meaning and significance of the Christian message are discovered in the light of a human experience through the working of the Holy Spirit. Where before there was only a human experience and the Christian message, now there is a third element effected by the Holy Spirit—namely, a deeper religious insight and discovery. The Spirit alone illumines the mind (the discovery) and moves the will (the response). This is precisely what distinguishes catechetics from every other academic discipline.

In the West, prone as we are to categorize knowledge, we left little room for the Holy Spirit, who works where He wills and as He wills. Again and again and again, He breaks up structures that life might live. The new catechetical process puts the Holy Spirit at the heart of itself. Hence the process is often called charismatic. Without the Spirit, there can be no discovery. If there is no discovery, there is no learning. If there is no learning, there is no responding—no change of life. That is why the witness of the teacher, the witness of the Christian community, prayer, and Eucharistic celebrations are so very, very important—these open up the student to the workings of the Holy Spirit. The parent plants, the teacher waters, but only the Spirit gives the growth.

Response will follow spontaneously, as the applause does after a fine performance on stage, or naturally, as when "tears from eyelids start."

The second point about response is that it is not always visible or immediate. At first it is *interior:* a deepening of some truth of faith, a burgeoning of that truth into a value. This is a lifelong process.

William James once wrote that interior feelings can be reinforced by exterior actions. A smile makes it easier to be happy. A kneeling posture facilitates praying. So to reaffirm the internal growing values, the new texts employ exterior activities. They publicly proclaim the heart movements stirred up in a lesson by a liturgy, as it were, of song or dance or silence or celebration.

CHART II

Old Process (Passive)	—	PRESENT A TRUTH	MEMORIZE IT	ACCEPT IT
New Process (Active)	PROBE LIFE EXPERIENCE	HEAR CHRISTIAN MESSAGE	DISCOVER	RESPOND

Therefore, in the new catechetical process there are four elements:

HUMAN EXPERIENCE

CHRISTIAN MESSAGE

DISCOVERING

RESPONDING

There are three actors: the student, the teacher, and the Holy Spirit.

To exemplify the process once more, let us recall the experience of the apostles themselves. For years they walked with Christ. This was their human experience. During those years, Christ taught them. This was the Christian message. The experience and the message, by themselves, were not enough for the apostles. On the night Christ died, they all fled away. The disciples on the way to Emmaus were a picture of the disappointment and disillusionment they all felt. For them there was no interaction between their human experience and the message of Christ until they were made to discover the meaning of the message in that experience. This discovery happened when the Holy Spirit came upon them on Pentecost Sunday. On that Sunday the apostles realized for the first time that the Man with whom they had been involved was God all along; that they had been walking and talking and witnessing the words and deeds of God Himself. They could hardly believe it. They were drunk with ecstatic joy. Their response was to burst out of the upper room and proclaim the Word.

By understanding this catechetical process, parents and teachers ought to see its relevancy. The new catechetics integrates life and religion. That is why life situations play so large a part in the new texts and methods. The experiences of life are given meaning through the message, illuminated by the Holy Spirit.

Catechetics: A Process

In the Old Testament the Exodus was to the People of God what the Incarnation is to Christianity. Some people have always viewed this event as though it were a spectacular extravaganza—a Cecil B. DeMille production. They assume that the Hebrews saw all along that God was intervening in their escape from slavery, that the event was obviously miraculous to them. The reality was not at all like that.

At the time of the Exodus, something unusual did happen. The people had been slaves. A clever leader, Moses, comes to their rescue. With him they gain their freedom, and they escape into the desert. The Hebrews were happy just to get free. For them, the event was hardly a religious one at all. God had spoken only to Moses. Naturally, Moses confided in his own flesh and blood, his brother and sister—Aaron and Miriam. Thus when the Hebrews had escaped through the Sea of Reeds, it was Miriam who put two and two together and discovered the hand of God behind this event. She began singing, "God has freed us. . . ." But the people had to be taught by God at Mount Sinai the significance of this event—that He was behind it. That was why He repeated so often, "I am the Lord, your God, who brought you out of the land of Egypt. . . ."

In this event we see the catechetical process. The "new" catechetics begins with a life experience. In this particular instance, it was degrading slavery and the escape from it. The message was the revelation through Moses to the Hebrews that this was the work of God. In learning that the Exodus was the work of God, the Hebrews began to discover who God is. They saw that God is involved in life—in their lives in particular. They learned that God wanted them to be free and that God is a God of love, One who cares. They learned this from experience, from something that had happened to them. Their response was to accept the pact that God wished to make with them—to become His people. To reinforce this commitment, they talked about what God had done in the Exodus, sang about it, celebrated it, until gradually their lives were changed. This is the basic process of religious education.

Too often we box ourselves in by situating all scriptural events in the frame of reference of the miraculous. We do not live in the miraculous; hence, if we overemphasize the miraculous in salvation history, we automatically exclude ourselves. That is why God never worked a miracle so obviously miraculous that it left no room for faith. Christ was a sign of contradiction, for many of His deeds could be challenged. In our times, Schweitzer claimed to have proved that none of Christ's miracles were miraculous. The real miracle is that God is involved in the

Catechetics: A Process

ordinary experiences of everyday living.

So the catechetical process for the Chosen People began with a human experience: slavery and liberation from it. Next, Moses proclaimed the message revealed to him that God was the one who had freed them: "I am the Lord, your God, who brought you out of the land of Egypt." The people themselves discovered the relationship between the human experience and the message: it told them volumes about this God of their fathers. So they responded with song and a covenant with God.

All catechesis nowadays employs these four steps: human experience, revealed message, discovery and response. That is why the new catechetics is called a process. It is more than giving the revealed message as in the old catechisms. It is more complex.

A human experience is generally used to launch a lesson in the new catechetics. God takes us as we are and from where we are. So does the new catechetics. In the fourth grade *Come to the Father,* for instance, the subject is the life of Christ. Because children tend to imitate their elders at this level, Christ's life is presented as seen through the eyes of ten adult witnesses. One of these who saw Christ was Matthew.

This lesson on the witness of Matthew begins with an exploration of the human experience of being welcomed and not being welcomed. A teacher may ask questions like this: "When kids were choosing sides for a game, were you ever left out?" "How did you feel?" "Were you ever punished by being sent to bed?" "Do you know of some people who have never been welcomed?" "What makes a person feel welcome?" "What makes him feel unwelcome?" And so on, and on.

This is what is meant by saying the new catechetics is experiential: it takes a human experience and probes it. It is precisely in this area of the process that there is room for discussion, analysis, stimulation, listening, interaction and learner involvement. It is especially here that teaching is dialectic, inductive and inquisitive. "Teaching is a sharing process. . . . It is intercommunication. It includes the collision, the creative interaction of minds."

I think confusion arises about the new catechetical method when people conclude that probing a human experience is the entire teaching process. They must realize that this is only the first step in the process, that it is not geared to teaching a doctrine so much as to probing an experience that ultimately will lead to the discovery of the meaning of the Christian message. Students want teachers who will make them think. Step one of the process does just that.

The second step in the process is the message. The Christian message is first of all brief. To Moses it was, "I am the Lord, your God, who led you out of the land of Egypt." For the Christian it can be summarized in the two commandments: the love of God and the love of neighbor. Even when this Christian message is elaborated, it can be capsuled in a catechism. So there is no need for an agenda anxiety. The entire Christian faith need not be packed into a child's head before the eighth grade.

In this phase teaching can be didactic and deductive. But here again, the proclamation of the good news must not be nagged into the child.

Ram it in, jam it in;
Students' heads are hollow.

Ram it in, jam it in;
There's plenty more to follow.

Rather the message should be suggested gently, quietly. All the teacher is doing is setting the stage for the Holy Spirit to go to work. In the fourth grade lesson on Matthew, after probing the human experience of being welcomed and not being welcomed, the teacher has the student read the call of Levi from the Gospel—just that, little more.

The third step is the discovery. Israel spent her whole history discovering who her redeeming God really and truly was. Each generation discovered a bit more about Him. To Abraham, God was an all-powerful Being. To Moses, He was a Person with a name. Then each of the prophets unfolded one aspect of His personality: His holiness, His love, His mercy, His justice, His forgiveness, etc.

In our fourth grade lesson, the Holy Spirit will help the child discover a bit more about Jesus. Nobody welcomed Levi, but Jesus did! Discovering this will implant in the child's heart trust in Jesus. A truth about Jesus will become a value—something very personal and subjective to the discoverer.

This phase of the catechetical process demands that teachers be men and women of faith, that the community be one of faith, that the Eucharist be frequently celebrated, that prayers be prayed. Commenting on the words of Samuel—"Speak, Lord, your servant hears"—Thomas à Kempis remarked in *The Imitation of Christ* (3:2):

"Let not Moses nor any of the prophets speak to me, but speak Thou rather, O Lord, God . . . for

Thou alone can perfectly instruct men, but they without Thee avail me nothing.

"They may indeed sound forth words, but they give not the spirit. They speak well, but if Thou be silent they do not set the heart on fire.

"They deliver the letter, but Thou discloseth the sense. They publish mysteries, but Thou explainest the meaning of the thing signified.

"They declare the commandments, but Thou enablest us to keep them. They show the way, but Thou givest strength to walk in it. They cry out with words, but Thou givest understanding to hearing.

"Let not then Moses speak to me, but Thou. . . ."

The final phase of the catechetical process is the response. For Israel it was accepting a covenant with God. For the fourth grade class it could be a party, like Levi's to celebrate his call. To this class party everyone would be welcomed—no one unwelcomed.

The response is generally a community exteriorization of the interior discovery—a "liturgy." An act, or ritual, expresses an interior feeling and usually strengthens it. That is why people often kneel when they pray—the posture helps. The response can be a song, a silent prayer, a celebration, an activity. When done in community, these responses have even greater force.

The new catechetical process, therefore, situates religious education where it belongs—in the present! So often we tend to relegate God and His will to the past or to the future. If to the past, He becomes irrelevant. If to the future, we become apathetic. The new catechetics probes an everyday experience to produce a now-response.

Films in the Catechetical Process

Christ commanded the apostles and their successors to "teach all nations" and to be "the light of the world." During His life on earth, Christ showed Himself to be the perfect Communicator, for the medium was the message: the Word was made flesh. He used what means of social communication were available in His time. Should the modern apostle not avail himself of all opportunities for announcing the good news offered by the modern media, he would indeed be suspect of not obeying Christ's command (#126, Pastoral Instruction on *Social Communication*, 5/23/71).

The media are invaluable helps for Christian education. They make the services of experts in religious teaching available. They have at their command the technical know-how to present religious teaching attractively and in contemporary style (*Idem*, #129).

Perhaps the media exerting the strongest influence on education, knowledge, culture and leisure is the film. It is a very effective means of expressing contemporary attitudes, views and interpretations of life and of increasing audience participation. Hence this medium should find greater use in pastoral action (*Idem,* #142).

Religious education films may be divided into three classes: (1) experiential; (2) catechetical; and (3) instructional.

The *experiential* film is any film that aims at creating a feeling for or against a way of life or some moral or spiritual value. It offers an experience without comment, like "Brian's Song" which sang of the unique friendship between Brian Piccolo and Gale Sayers. It may or may not have been produced for religious education. All great art has religious truth in it. But the experiential film also has Madison Avenue in it. It shows a life experience to create an audience reaction. Another such film would be "The Red Balloon" by Lamorisse: an Academy Award winner about a boy in Paris and a balloon.

The experiential film is not just an ice-breaker to get discussion going. It does that, but more. The common experience which a class has had from seeing it becomes the topic of discussion almost as much as the film itself.

Such a film can be diagnostic, a pre-testing, to discover how a class feels about a certain theme, such as war, peace, racism, poverty, and so on.

For instance, in the Choose Life Series, religious education is treated thematically. Should a teacher, for example, desire to sound out the students' attitudes toward racism in the theme of People, an experiential film could serve the purpose. The film "Let the Rain Settle It" is the story of a chance encounter between two young boys, one white and one black. The two boys are thrown together for twenty-

Films in the Catechetical Process 45

four hours. A discussion of this film will expose race attitudes and student backgrounds. Thus it will clue the teacher as to what points have to be made in handling this specific lesson. In addition, the film will dispose the class for the lesson. It will plunge them deep into it before they even realize it is a "class."

"A good film discussion," wrote Sister Elise, "leads people to talk about themselves and their attitudes toward life; to share a little bit of their hidden selves never before shared, to shed some of the mask, to tear down a little of the wall. A discussion that starts and ends talking only about a film has gone nowhere" (*A New Direction in High School Religious Education,* p. 57).

A second kind of film is the *catechetical* film. This film is made specifically for the classroom and is based on the catechetical process. It presents a human experience and a Christian message, intending to lead students to discovering that message and responding to it. Such films, therefore, ought to be analyzed along the fourfold lines of the catechetical process: human experience, Christian message, discovery, and response.

Thus the catechetical film will center primarily on the life experience, as it should, for the life-situation is generally the major portion of the catechetical lesson. The teacher's task is to have the students probe this film experience. The procedure is to examine what the film says literally—to glean the first, spontaneous reaction to it. Before arriving at the fuller meaning of a Scripture passage, one must first understand what it says in its literal context. The same is true here. One starts with having the class discuss the obvious: the story of the film.

Consider, for instance, a film called "Revelation," produced by Panfilm. As in all its other productions, Panfilm here follows the catechetical process closely. The life experience is an obvious one: it is the story of a blind man—in the first half of the film he is blind, in the second half he receives his sight. Quite simple, quite obvious. And that is exactly where the teacher should begin probing. Such questions could be asked: "What was the blind man doing?" "How did he feel?" "What do you think he was wishing for?" "What clues did the lyrics of the Ray Repp's songs give about the blind man's feelings?" "What happened to the blind man?" "Does the song tell anything about his feelings now?" "About his relationship to the world?" "To others?" "To himself?" "Why was the shroud of Milan used?" After the blind man had recovered his sight, a shot of another blind man with a seeing-eye dog was given. "Why was this done?" "How did you feel in seeing this blind man?"

The second step for the teacher is to present the Christian message. In a catechetical film this can be found either in the title, sometimes in the lyrics, in a background newscast, or from some remark by one of the actors themselves. The title "Revelation" hints, even before one sees the film, what the Christian message might be. The film itself becomes even more explicit by using Scripture: the story of the blind man on the road to Jericho (Mk. 10:46ff.).

The third stage in studying a catechetical film is crucial, because it involves the all-important step of discovery. Unless the student discovers the meaning of the Christian message in the light of the human experience, he has not learned. The skilled teacher, therefore, stands back in the discussion and remains as neutral as possible. He is chary of imposing, or precipitously revealing, the discoveries he himself has made from previous viewings of the film. Instead he stimulates, prods the students to probe, guides them along the way, and enables them to discover the meaning of the Christian message in the light of the human experience related in the film.

In the film "Revelation," how wonderful if the student can realize and discover, by this process, that God's Word is to the spirit of man what sight is to a blind man and what light is to a man who has eyes to see. How wonderful if the student perceives that as sight enabled the blind man to belong to the community of men, so the faith and love community, which is the Church, is built up by the insight and the light emanating from the Word of God.

The ultimate aim of all catechetics, and so of the film, is to evoke a response in the student. This need not be any present commitment, but merely a deepening of the faith—of a truth emerging as a value for the student. It may be no more than beginning to put more value on the Word of God, especially the Liturgy of the Word at Mass. Perhaps it may be an experience, through the film, of the happiness in this Word of God: "Happy is the man who trusts in the Lord our God." If the student has gotten only this—an appreciation of God's Word, a deep, inner resolve to be a bit more open to it, happy over it—this is indeed achievement enough.

A film like "Revelation" might well be shown more than once. Hurry is the bane of all learning. The catechetical film can be contemplated, meditated upon, shown again and again. Seed-sowing is always fruitful (Is. 55:11). Trust the Holy Spirit to work. He will give it growth—maybe only years later, after the student has left the classroom for the arena of the world. But He will, in His own good time. (For an analysis of other catechetical films, see Appendix 2.)

The third and final kind of film is not a movie at all, but the frame-by-frame filmstrip. The filmstrip is generally the instructional film. Often it is produced simply to present a truth. It addresses the intellect alone. Its function is to teach, not to change a person. Information, not formation, is usually its sole goal.

In using the filmstrip, there are two dangers. First, it may be used as the message and not the medium. It would be wrong to focus on the filmstrip (and on films, for that matter) with a remark such as: "Students, we have something special today." The filmstrip is not a gimmick to gain attention; it is an aid to the lesson and only that. The important thing is the lesson. The filmstrip happens to be used only because it can introduce a lesson, help teach it, or help students review it. Religious education must not deteriorate into entertainment. Students must be more than spectators.

The second danger is that paradoxically the student may not see the filmstrip he is watching. He may just be looking at it, with his mind miles away. To make certain the student will see the filmstrip, a true-false test could be prepared and handed out before viewing the strip. The students answer the questions as the film progresses. After the viewing the teacher runs down the list of questions, polling the group for answers. Such a procedure promotes attention even to mediocre filmstrips.

Twenty-Third Publications offers a filmstrip "Finding a Conscience To Follow." The strip is meant to help parents establish norms that are reasonable for their children. Before showing this to a parent group preparing their children for First Penance, the following true-false quiz could be handed out and discussed after the viewing.

FINDING A CONSCIENCE TO FOLLOW

1. The journey of man is one of building and of tearing down.   T   F

2. Life is a search for a new law and a new order.   T   F

3. We are all in search of an escape, like Lucy.   T   F

4. The answering-service church has gone out of business.   T   F

5. Laws never change.   T   F

6. The law serves and is a guide to help us live with others and with ourselves in the presence of God.   T   F

7. To be true to oneself is the path to happiness and fulfillment.   T   F

8. Being true to oneself means being conscious of who we are in relation to others.   T   F

9. The law of life is our consciousness of others, which is to say our conscience.   T   F

10. Others, like Snoopy, help us to confront the truth of ourselves.   T   F

11. Conscience is not a voice: it is the capacity to relate to others as we are.   T   F

12. Awareness of others shows how we are all caught up in the human and inhuman condition, how all men share in a common struggle.   T   F

13. To overcome evil is not a matter of seeking a world elsewhere: it is making the best of what we have where we are.

14. Following laws gives us new life.   T   F

15. Man's will is a muscle he applies in choosing an appealing good.   T   F

16. The will is man's capacity to make responsible decisions about his relationships with the human condition.   T   F

17. Each one can choose his own family, but he cannot choose how he wishes to live in relation to his own family and the family of man.   T   F

18 To be or not to be is the question of every man.   T   F

19. To choose freely how to be does not come easy automatically.   T   F

20. Freedom of choice involves picking from only two possibilities: to keep or break the law.   T   F

21. Free choice involves availability of options and the capacity to recognize the consequences of this choice.   T   F

22. Without options, free choice is a depressing burden.   T   F

23. The parental task is to teach the child only one way of choosing: to choose right over wrong.   T   F

Films in the Catechetical Process

24. Parents must help the child recognize and choose from among available options, to recognize the consequences of different choices, and to be aware of their relationships with others.   T   F

25. The main concern of parents is not to teach children how to avoid evil, but to instill the desire to find new ways of living in this world.   T   F

A film or filmstrip is a waste of precious time in religious education unless the teacher prepares himself for presenting it, prepares the class for seeing it, and discusses it after they have viewed it.

Catechetical Aim: Conscience Formation

Anyone discussing conscience formation, like a good philosopher, ought to make a distinction between conscience and forming conscience.

Conscience is the intellect passing judgment on the goodness or badness of an action here and now to be done. If the action is good, conscience prompts one to choose it; if bad, it prods one not to choose it. These proddings and promptings are called the "dictates" or "voice" of conscience. Conscience, therefore, involves two acts: judgment and choice. Since it does, conscience formation must address itself to both the mind and the will. The ever-present danger in conscience formation is to see it as the development of either the mind or the will without any reference of the one to the other.

A catechist who sees conscience formation only as informing the mind would reduce religious education to *indoctrination*. Indoctrination means informing the student about right and wrong, packing his head with knowledge, and requiring no judgment on his part. Religious education in this concept would be a process of simply learning questions and the appropriate answers. Catechetics becomes only an answering service—no need for judgment or reflection. The errors in this approach lie in the fact that the ability to judge is not being developed and the will is being totally neglected.

On the other hand, a catechist who sees conscience formation only as the programming of behavior would reduce religious education to *behaviorism*. The success of the program depends on the students' behavior. The catechist believes that if he "makes" the student act according to set standards, all will be well. Bernard Haring labeled this method as forming conscience through imperatives: "Do this." "Don't do that." The flaw with the behavioral approach is that it does not touch the will, for it does not involve choice. Prisoners in a prison behave well, but mere conformity to rules is no guarantee of rehabilitation.

For the same reason, the commercial approach, that of offering rewards, does not form conscience. A rewards-only approach, like a bribe, can adulterate motivation. The Pharisee in our Lord's parable prayed, fasted twice a week and gave tithes of all he possessed. Yet he was not good. Virtue is much more than mere behavior!

Insofar as conscience is a reasoned judgment, it needs to be informed. Insofar as it is a choice, it must be free. Unless it is both of these, conscience becomes nothing more than a feeling: something followed much as a man follows a wheelbarrow.

One phase of conscience formation, therefore, is to develop the mind to conform to the mind of

Catechetical Aim: Conscience Formation 55

Christ: to teach what is the right thing to do and to teach what is the right motive for doing it. This task is relatively easy, since it consists in the presentation of the truths of Faith. What is difficult here is the *manner of presentation:* the teachings of the Church must be presented persuasively enough to move one to evaluate his own judgments in the light of those teachings. The presentation must encourage one to think—to think about motives and values! Yet at the same time it must preserve his freedom of choice.

This freedom of choice, the second and more difficult phase of conscience formation, is the heart of it. For the object here is to strengthen the will not only to choose what it has learned to be the right thing, but to choose it consistently and to act from the right motive.

How can one be taught to do this? By developing the habit of making good choices. Habit is a consistent way of acting acquired through repetition. We speak of a good golfer, a good bowler, a good tennis player. Do we mean a person who makes a good shot now and then or bowls a good game now and then? No. We mean somebody who consistently makes good shots. He can make bad ones, too. But his eyes, nerves, and muscles have been so trained by constant practice that he can now be relied upon. He has developed a certain habit, a tone or quality, and it is there even when he is not playing.

So, forming conscience means fostering the habit of making good choices, so that one can be relied upon to choose good most of the time.

A choice, by its nature, must be free. Freedom requires that there be alternatives of equal value, any one of which may be freely selected. To offer a child a choice between two alternatives, one of which is a serious sin, allows no choice, because no one is free to choose an evil like sin. Therefore, when choice is not given and action is forced, far from developing conscience, a rebel or a hypocrite is created. That is why the "Gospel spirit of freedom and charity" must pervade religious education.

In summary, conscience formation demands: (1) informing conscience, and (2) forming it.

We inform conscience by presenting what is the right thing to do, and by showing what is the right motive for doing it.

We form conscience by disposing one to choose the right thing consistently, and to act for the right reason.

"The forming of the Christian conscience of children or youth consists, first and foremost, in illuminating their minds concerning Christ's desires, His law and His way, and in addition in influencing their souls insofar as this can be done from the outside, in order that they may execute the divine Will freely and constantly. This is the highest duty of education" (Pius XII, 3/23/52).

CHART III

Conscience Involves	Conscience Formation Involves	Dangers
Judgment	1. Teaching Christian principles 2. Stimulating thinking re motives, values	Indoctrination
Choice	3. Freedom: to choose 4. Good example: to choose rightly	Behaviorism

Catechetical Aim: Conscience Formation 57

In practice, how do we form conscience? Again another distinction is in order, based on the age-development of the child: pre-school, pre-adolescent and adolescent.

For the Pre-School Child

Conscience is best formed through parental example and the family spirit in the home. In the book *Will Religion Make Sense to Your Child?* Larsen and Galvin write to parents: "Just as your children are 'vacuum cleaners' of ideas, attitudes and values in regard to everything else, so too, they absorb Christianity. Children are blotters! You have been and ARE teaching them more about Christianity by your living example than any number of words you, or anyone else, will ever speak to them." Earlier, they write: "Kids pick up everything, especially attitudes. They are 'learning' on a far-deeper level than just word-communication. They are picking up your attitudes toward life, toward the Church, toward the Mass, toward each other." So ineradicable are these home "lessons" that most couples adopting children will not take them if they are over two years old. It is felt that the child's future growth has already been determined. He can be taken out of the home, but the home cannot be taken out of him.

For the Pre-Adolescent

We best form conscience by making good *alluring*. This involves reversing the concept of scandal. Scandal is not simply doing something bad in the presence of another. It is doing something bad in his presence in such a way as to make the evil so alluring that he chooses to do that very thing.

In conscience formation we must reverse this process. We must make the good so alluring to the child that he will choose to do it.

Therefore, for the pre-adolescent, the most important thing in conscience formation is again EXAMPLE—children are lovers, not philosophers. Conscience is formed through personal relationships: the teacher's example and the example given by the community of the home, of the school, of the Church and of society.

The Teacher. The child learns religion best not so much from good textbooks or all kinds of media, but basically from the example of good teachers. Children learn best from prayerful teachers who themselves love the Faith and cherish it. "Outstanding human and Christian qualities in the catechists will be able to do more to produce successes than will the methods selected" (*General Catechetical Directory* #71; see also #114).

The child also learns from the teacher's instruction, which itself is concerned with the example of persons. Thus in grades one to three, the *Come to the Father* approach to religious education is personal. The lessons are based on the Persons of the Trinity and their relationships to each other and to the child. In grades four to six, Christ's life and teachings are revealed by the words and example of those who had seen the Lord.

The Home. Parents educate, not so much by being teachers, as by being parents. Parental example and

Catechetical Aim: Conscience Formation

the family spirit in the home are of superlative importance, for CHILDREN LEARN WHAT THEY LIVE.

If a child lives with criticism,
   He learns to condemn.
If a child lives with hostility,
   He learns to fight . . .
If a child lives with tolerance,
   He learns to be patient.
If a child lives with encouragement,
   He learns to have confidence.
If a child lives with praise,
   He learns to appreciate.
If a child lives with fairness,
   He learns justice.
If a child lives with security,
   He learns to have faith . . .
If a child lives with acceptance and friendship,
   He learns to find love in the world.

Parents are teachers always, whether they realize it or not. A father buying a movie ticket for his son lied about the boy's age. The child's protest was cut short by a knowing wink from his dad. Should the father be surprised to hear the boy's remark: "Gee, Dad, you're smart. When I grow up, I hope I can cheat like you"?

The School. In pre-adolescence, values are absorbed from the example of the school community. There "an atmosphere enlivened by the Gospel spirit of freedom and charity" must prevail (*Christian Education,* #8). Freedom is essential for choices, and charity is essential for teaching responsibility to others.

The Church. The liturgy has been renewed precisely to create a worshiping community whose example would also teach and impart values.

Society. Movies, TV, press are such powerful influences for good or evil that no parent can be indifferent to the example they give.

For Adolescents

Conscience is best formed by value education. But *what are values,* and *how do we arrive at them?*

A value is something that is important to one's life —something one has thought through, and freely chosen from alternatives. A value represents something one esteems so highly that it affects his life: he lives for it, he would die for it. The problem of religious education is to make what is a value to us—the Christian faith—become a thing of value for the student. Not just something to learn, but something to esteem, to love—yes, to value even more than life itself.

We arrive at value by a seven-step process (see Appendix 1) according to Sidney B. Simon in *Values and Teachings.* The basic steps are the first two in the process: *thinking a thing out* and *freely choosing it.* We must examine all the angles before choosing something so that we know exactly what we are doing and we do it because we want to. This thinking process involves becoming fully conscious of who we are and of who we are in relation to others and to God.

Our Lord taught the same thing. If a man is going to build a watchtower in his vineyard, he first calcu-

Catechetical Aim: Conscience Formation 61

lates the cost to see if he has money enough to build it. Or if a general were going off to battle, he would first consider, before engaging the enemy, whether or not he had a chance of success (Lk. 14:25-33). Christ said that we must think things out!

That is why, especially for teenagers, prayerful meditation is a necessity for growth in faith, for faith to become a precious value. Meditation is ruminating on the truths of faith, in relation to everyday experiences. When one discovers, under the light of the Holy Spirit, that a truth of faith has a particular meaning for life, then he perceives it as good and is impelled to choose it.

The response of such choices builds up the habit of choosing good, which is the formation of conscience.

The General Catechetical Directory

Historical Background

In April, 1971, the General Catechetical Directory was released. The Directory is the response to the request made by the Second Vatican Council in the Decree on the Bishops' Pastoral Office: "Another directory should be composed with respect to the catechetical instruction of the Christian people, and should deal with the fundamental principles of such instruction, its arrangement, and the composition of books on the subject" (#44).

In 1967, Pope Paul VI entrusted the drawing up of the Directory to the Sacred Congregation for the Clergy. The very first question to be settled before working on this document was whether or not it would be better to prepare a general catechism instead of a directory. The idea of a general catechism was dropped on the grounds that a catechism for the universal Church would end up as more a basic statement of doctrine than a catechism. A catechism is specific: it explains the content of faith to a particular audience. But a directory is more general: it seeks to give directions to all the activity of the ministry of the Word, and particularly to that activity which brings a believing people to maturity of faith.

Once that fundamental question was resolved, Jean Cardinal Villot, then Prefect of the Sacred Congregation for the Clergy, presented to the First Synod of Bishops the criteria to be followed in drawing up the document.

Early in 1968 questionnaires went out to all Episcopal Conferences regarding the nature and purpose of catechesis and the criteria for handling doctrinal content and incorporating catechetical activity in the pastoral mission of the Church. The answers submitted were examined by an international commission of seven experts. In October, 1968, this commission drew up a first draft of the Directory and presented it to a Plenary Session of the Sacred Congregation for the Clergy.

Revising the text according to the suggestions made at this Session, the commission then sent it for examination to all Episcopal Conferences early in 1969. When the reactions of the Bishops were received this second time, the commission went to work on the definitive text.

After this was finished, the Directory was examined in 1970-71 by a special commission of theologians and the Sacred Congregation for the Doctrine of the Faith. The reason for this was to insure a balanced treatment in the Directory: catechists would naturally focus on people, those to be catechized; theologians would focus on the deposit of faith.

On April 11, 1971, the Directory was published with the approval of Pope Paul VI (cf.

Oss. Rom. 7/11/71).

The Directory

The Directory is divided into six parts with an Addendum (Appendix). Though the approach in the Directory is positive and pastoral, the first half of it is devoted to resolving a tension which is at the center of the catechetical renewal.

This tension is generated by two facts: our ever-changing culture and our never-changing Faith. The problem is how to keep the Faith intact and at the same time be contemporary.

So Part I in the Directory explores the contemporary situation in the world and in the Church. Then in Parts II and III, the Directory presents the sources and the content of the Faith. In Part I the Directory says, "This is what the situation is. This demands changes in communication." In Parts II and III the Directory says, "This is what the Faith is. This demands fidelity to content." So what does the Directory do to resolve the problem?

It steers a middle course between our changing culture and our unchanging Faith. It avoids both extremes. First it avoids the extreme position of those who would ignore modern cultural changes. These are the "concrete" catechists, those so hardened in their opinions that they will not budge, will make no concessions, not even in so peripheral an element as the *manner* of presenting the Faith. These catechists are like the servant in the parable who buried his talent. By ignoring cultural changes, and keeping the Faith in the molds of an outdated culture, they preserve the Faith intact indeed, but they do this by burying it! They bypass society, and society passes them by.

The other extreme is that of the "capricious" catechists—those who are so eager to meet modern man on his own terms that they sacrifice the Faith. They change not only the manner of expression, but the Faith itself. They are like the prodigal son who squandered his inheritance and fed on the husks of swine.

The Directory strives to avoid this Scylla and Charybdis. Change there must be—that's what Part I says. But this change must not be in the substance of the doctrine but only in the manner of expression —that's what Parts II and III are saying. How this can be done—that's what the rest of the Directory says. Thus:

Part I: The situation in the world and in the Church calls for change.

Part II: But in ministering the Word, whether by evangelization (to win others to the Faith) or by catechizing (to instruct in the Faith) or by liturgy (to celebrate the Faith) or by theology (to investigate the Faith), the minister is not free to go off on his own: he must reflect and echo God's revelation contained in Scripture and Tradition.

Part III: The Christian message must lead to maturity of faith. Again, there is no room for whimsy or electicism: the message must be presented in its completeness.

Part IV: This is to be done by no one method, for communication varies with persons, places and times. In general, however, both the inductive (the discovery method) and the deductive (the lecture

The General Catechetical Directory

method) and definitions can be used, drawing especially on the Holy Spirit and life experiences.

Part V: The best structure to follow is to teach according to different age groups. Adult catechesis is most important because adults can be led to the maturity of faith, which is the aim of all catechetics, and because adults can in turn become the catechists of the young.

Part VI: Episcopal Conferences must apply the general principles and declarations in the Directory to their specific countries and needs.

Addendum: The Church reaffirms the value of the traditional practice of having a child receive the sacrament of Penance before First Communion. However, experimentation by Bishops is permitted with the approval of Rome.

method and definitions can be used, drawing especially on the Holy Spirit and life experience.

Part F. The best format to follow is to teach according to different age groups. A full catechesis is most important for young adults, to be led to the maturity of faith, which is the aim of all catechesis, and if young adults can in turn become the catechists of the young.

Part K. Episcopal Conferences must apply the general principles, and determinations, in the Directory with specific country's and needs.

Catena (q). The Church reaffirms the value of the traditional practice of having a bit of receive the sacrament of Penance before First Communion. However, experimentation by Bishops is permitted with the prior verbal licence.

APPENDIX 1

The General Catechetical Directory has this to say about definitions:

"The advantages of the inductive method . . . must in no way lead to a forgetting of the need for the usefulness of formulas.

"Formulas permit the thoughts of the mind to be expressed accurately, are appropriate for a correct exposition of the Faith, and, when committed to memory, help toward the firm possession of truth. Finally, they make it possible for a uniform way of speaking to be used among the faithful.

"Formulas are generally presented and explained when the lesson or inquiry has reached the point of synthesis" (#73).

The objections to the Baltimore Catechism as a textbook have often been transferred to the rejection of definitions. This is a *non sequitur* if ever there was one.

The Directory in the above quoted passage points out the advantages of definitions and so the importance of catechisms (#119). However, what is of superlative importance is the last paragraph. It says there that definitions should come at the end of a lesson, not at the beginning.

Definition is always the last step in the educative process. Only when one knows something well, can he define it. Yet the reverse is not necessarily true. It need not follow that to be able to define is to know what is defined. I used to tell my students not to let their study interfere with their education. Students can memorize answers and not know the answers.

The values of our Faith cannot become values to students through courses aimed at indoctrination or encompassing only the memory of definitions. Values become values to a student only after going through an educative process. Dr. Sidney Simon enumerated the seven steps necessary in this process: (1) thinking a thing out, (2) choosing it freely, (3) from alternatives, (4) acting on it, (5) not once but repeatedly, (6) prizing it, and (7) being willing to stand up for it publicly. Omit any one of these seven steps and the value does not really emerge as a value to the learner. A system of religious education based only on definitions violates much of this process and renders it exceedingly difficult to transmit religious values.

Recall how Christ first proclaimed the good news of salvation. He evoked from a few the response of faith. A community formed and grew. It pondered the message of Christ, lived it, celebrated it. And then in the last half of the first century, God inspired men to write down Christ's words and deeds as seen through the eyes of faith of the first Christian community. In other words, the primeval catechetical process was—first, the historical event (the Incarnation and the Redemption); second, the response of

Appendix 1

faith (the Christian community), and lastly, the formulation of that faith (the New Testament and the creeds). Note well that formulation, or definition, was the last step!

What was the first step? Conversion *(metanoia)*. The aim of the proclamation *(kerygma)* of Christ and His apostles was conversion, a basic change in men's lives. Once the basic commitment was made, instruction *(didache)* followed. After the instruction came entrance into the community by Baptism and Eucharist *(koinonia)*.

The great tragedy today is that too often the process is reversed for children. They are baptized first, then instructed, and then hopefully (?) converted. No wonder so many adolescents and adults "fall away" later on. Conversion must always be at the heart of catechetics.

APPENDIX 2

Three outstanding catechetical films on Revelation, Reconciliation, and Resurrection are produced by Panfilms, Catechetics Mission Project, 321 Broadway, New York, New York 10007.

Teleketics is another company producing excellent catechetical films. Write for a catalogue to Franciscan Communications Center, Teleketics Division, 1229 So. Santee Street, Los Angeles, California 90015.

All these films deal with religious education subjects in such a way that they will be relevant for a long time to come.

The following analyses of some basic catechetical films are given to demonstrate the skeletal facts a teacher should have about a film. Having some such outline, the teacher will be able to guide discussion and prevent it from running wild.

TITLE	HUMAN EXPERIENCE	CHRISTIAN MESSAGE	DISCOVERY	RESPONSE
R E V E L A T I O N (10 min.) Junior High through Adult	*Part 1:* A blind man walking a city street. Probe: 1. How did he feel? (Uncertain and alone) 2. What did he wish for? (Light and sight) *Part 2:* The same man walking a crowded city street, no longer blind. How did he feel now? (Joy, a sense of belonging)	Analyze title. The two Ray Repp songs. The Scripture read from Mk. 10:46ff.	Blindness can be spiritual (Jn. 9) as well as physical. Revelation, or God's Word, is like *sight* to the blind and *light* to the seeing (Mt. 13:14). As sight and light make community possible, so the Word of God builds community.	Joy. Openness to the Liturgy of the Word. Seeing fellow man in the new light of community.
R E C O N C I L I A T I O N (13 min.) Junior High through Adult	Boy playing soldier—and war clips. A man teaches the boy to play games—Pope Paul VI visits U.N. (Note the parallels with the Pentecost event.) Chanting the values and headliners of the 60's.	Analyze title. Song: "Silent Night"—Christ coming in joy to bring "peace on earth." Song: *"Veni Creator Spiritus"*—Christ sending the Holy Spirit, the God of Love.	Man can learn the ways of peace through other men: especially the Word made flesh. After 2,000 years of Christianity man still needs reconciling. The values shown in the headliners of the 60's must move toward justice, peace, life, love, Jesus Christ.	Be a peacemaker. Be more loving. Be Christlike!

TITLE	HUMAN EXPERIENCE	CHRISTIAN MESSAGE	DISCOVERY	RESPONSE
R E S U R R E C T I O N (12 min.) Junior High through Adult	A woman going to Mass early in the morning (the Holy Eucharist). Four human events narrated: 1. Assassination of King. 2. Assassination of Kennedy. 3. Vietnam battlefield. 4. Johnson halts bombing. The sacrament identified with each event: 1. Baptism. 2. Matrimony and Holy Orders. 3. Anointing of the sick (3 & 4). The triple refrain after each sacrament: 1. Music. 2. Ballet. 3. City at sunrise.	Analyze title Mary Magdalene's visit to tomb on Easter morn. Insights into the sacraments. Sacraments are: 1. encounters with the risen Christ (Eucharist). 2. events of joy (music). 3. means of transformation (ballerina). 4. calls to witness (sunrise in the city).	Sacraments touch us in the important events of our lives. The sacraments transform us because Christ is risen. Mary Magdalene found the empty tomb of the risen Christ; the woman at Mass found the risen Christ in the Eucharist.	*Thanks* that God is with us at every stage of life. *Joy* that we are transformed. SHOW THANKS AND JOY IN EVERYDAY LIFE, ESPECIALLY IN THE LITURGY OF THE WORD.

TITLE	HUMAN EXPERIENCE	CHRISTIAN MESSAGE	DISCOVERY	RESPONSE
B A P T I S M (8 min.) Elementary through Adult	Alfredo, a Mexican orphan tragically scarred by fire. For him the most important thing is to belong: to have a place to live, to love, to have a family to love. He stumbles on the "Hacienda" — a home of Little Brothers and Sisters. He sees that it is one vast family. He pleads to be adopted. His desire is put before the children, who answer "You are my brother."	Before the film, orientation and background are needed: "This is a parable which can be used to illuminate Baptism as the sacrament of belonging."	The Church is a family into which we are adopted by Baptism and all are made brothers and sisters. God wants us to live as a family.	To show our love for God our Father by accepting others as brothers — especially those most in need of love.
P E N A N C E (11 min.) Intermediate through Adult	A man injures a small girl in a car accident. His initial guilt and fear separate him from those he loves, and he isolates himself in self-pity. A psychiatrist makes him aware of his own responsibility. A deep sense of sorrow drives him to seek forgiveness from the injured child and her parents.	Before the film, again set the stage: "This is a parable that can be used to teach Penance as the sacrament of reconciliation and peace."	Effect of sin is alienation: the rupturing of relationships. Forgiveness is restoring relationships. Peace is the result. Asking forgiveness of one we have injured is the most natural thing in the world to do.	Avoid injuring anyone. If done, seek forgiveness.

TITLE	HUMAN EXPERIENCE	CHRISTIAN MESSAGE	DISCOVERY	RESPONSE
E U C H A R I S T (10 min.) Junior High through Adult	1. Four vignettes of everyday life with parallel liturgical actions: a. forgotten aged; b. poor family; c. lonely teenager; d. wounded soldier. 2. Sounds: a. heartbeat; b. folksong; c newscast. 3. Sights: a. planting and maturation of seeds; b. gathering and breaking of storm.	Orient viewers before showing the film by asking them to: a. note the four everyday experiences; b. see the parallel in the liturgical actions; c. try to read what the sights and sounds say; d. discover how the film shows the Eucharist as the sacrament of life.	All people need more than physical life. This more abundant life is to be found in the Eucharist which gives new life, unity, nourishment, healing, and joy.	We need life! We need love! We need joy! We need unity! All ought to seek the Eucharist: the fountain of life, love, joy, and unity.

TITLE	HUMAN EXPERIENCE	CHRISTIAN MESSAGE	DISCOVERY	RESPONSE
C O N F I R M A T I O N (11 min.) Intermediate through Junior High	Bobby Anderson, 12 years old, is preparing for confirmation. Bobby has a vivid imagination, like boys his age. The words "soldier of Christ" sends Bobby soaring off into flights of fantasy. He imagines himself as an astronaut, as feeding starving millions, as a U.N. delegate dispensing peace to the world. At the same time the prosaic realities of life at home keep intruding. Faced with an opportunity to live out his fantasies, he stops a fight, only to get turned off. He begins to realize what "strong and perfect Christian" means.	Confirmation is the sacrament calling us to give witness to our faith. To witness, a person must have understanding and strength (martyr). Confirmation, therefore gives the fullness of the Holy Spirit who enlightens the mind and strengthens the will.	Witness is to tell by word or deed what one believes. We need strength to live the faith in ordinary, everyday life—which is witness.	Live the faith from day to day in all things — great *and* small! Look for help to do this by daily prayer to the Holy Spirit.

TITLE	HUMAN EXPERIENCE	CHRISTIAN MESSAGE	DISCOVERY	RESPONSE
W I T N E S S (8 min.) Junior High through Adult	Six telespots: 1. Masks of man 2. A boy's man 3. Like father, like son. 4. Count your blessings. 5. I hate elevators. 6. Restricted neighborhood. Each spot is designed to be used independently.	Following each spot there is a brief scriptural quotation for reflection and discussion.	Everyday encounters can be transformed into moments of Christian witness by what we are, say and do.	1. Be real! Let your faith show. 2. Show your love: a father is someone to be with, to enjoy, discover, and share with. 3. Give good example. 4. Be concerned for others: witness is more than feeling — it is sharing. 5. Be kind to all, for we are brothers. 6. Stand up for what is right.